SHORT ON TIME

*How do I make time to lead
and learn as a principal?*

William
STERRETT

ASCD   Alexandria, VA USA

arias™

Website: www.ascd.org   www.ascdarias.org
E-mail: books@ascd.org

Printed in the United States of America. Cover art © 2013 by ASCD. ASCD publications present a variety of viewpoints. The views expressed or implied in this book should not be interpreted as official positions of the Association.

ASCD LEARN TEACH LEAD® and ASCD ARIAS™ are trademarks owned by ASCD and may not be used without permission. All other referenced trademarks are the property of their respective owners.

PAPERBACK ISBN: 978-1-4166-1815-7   ASCD product #SF114044

Also available as an e-book (see Books in Print for the ISBNs).

Library of Congress Cataloging-in-Publication Data
Sterrett, William.
  Short on time : how do I make time to lead and learn as a principal? / William Sterrett.
     pages cm. — (ASCD arias)
  Includes bibliographical references.
  ISBN 978-1-4166-1815-7 (pbk. : alk. paper) 1. School principals—
Professional relationships. I. Title.
  LB2831.9.S74 2013
  371.2'012—dc23

                                                        2013034063

21 20 19 18 17 16 15 14 13   1 2 3 4 5 6 7 8 9 10

SHORT ON TIME

How do I make time to lead and learn as a principal?

It's About Time.. 1

A Time for Managing Priorities 3

A Time for Maximizing Learning..................................... 13

A Time for Collaborative Growth 27

Making Time 38

Acknowledgments... 39

Encore 41

References 47

Related Resources... 48

About the Author 49

Want to earn a free ASCD Arias e-book?
Your opinion counts! Please take 2–3 minutes to give
us your feedback on this publication. All survey
respondents will be entered into a drawing to
win an ASCD Arias e-book.

Please visit
www.ascd.org/ariasfeedback

Thank you!

It's About Time

If only I had the time. How often do school principals hear this phrase from their hurried colleagues? Educators' sincere desire to do more, learn more, and engage more continually runs up against the realities of the frenetic, ever-changing world of teaching and learning.

I wish I could reach Benjamin better and see him more engaged. How is this possible, with so many other student needs to meet?

I would love to read that new book and apply a new perspective to my work. Who really has time to read, digest, and apply emerging ideas and best practices when so much is demanding our attention right this minute?

It would be great to log on to my Professional Learning Network (PLN) and collaborate with others. Despite our best intentions, exhaustion often trumps professional learning goals at the end of a busy day.

Today's educators are more stressed out than ever before. *The MetLife Survey of the American Teacher* (2013) examined the perspectives of teachers and principals across the United States and found some discouraging trends:

- Teacher job satisfaction has dropped by 23 points since 2008—its lowest level in 25 years.
- Principal job satisfaction has dropped by 9 points in the same period.

- The responsibilities of school leadership have changed significantly in recent years, leading to a job that principals say has become too complex and highly stressful.
- Half of all teachers function in formal leadership roles, yet few desire to become principals (although half are interested in a hybrid role that would include some teaching).

We are living in a time of sweeping curricular shifts and demographic changes. Uncertainties abound regarding educational funding and policy. Innovation *inside* the classroom and access to resources and perspectives *outside* the classroom hold unprecedented potential and promise for teaching and learning. We sorely need leadership in our schools. We must teach, learn, collaborate, and lead— together. Schools cannot be powered by a hard-working few or count on a small core to "show the way" to success.

Fostering ingenuity and innovation while maximizing student learning require deliberate planning and targeted action. In my 2011 ASCD book *Insights into Action*, I focused on practical action steps that effective school leaders take to realize success. Here, I want to build on that work by showing principals how making the most of the time allotted to us can lead to even greater success. In this era of unknowns, we must focus on maximizing the one predictable resource that is given to us each day: it's about *time*.

Reading *Short on Time* will help you take action and realize change in your school and professional life. You will gain insights into specific steps that you can apply to the context in which you serve. These action steps involve teaching, innovating, and leading. They require planning, action, and reflection.

Time is a limited resource, but it is the most equitably distributed resource. We get 24 hours of it each day. Let's use it well.

A Time for Managing Priorities

Principal Dwight Carter does not have a moment to spare. Now in his sixth year of leading Gahanna Lincoln High School, located on the outskirts of Columbus, Ohio, Carter maintains relationships with over 2,300 students and 200 staff members. Carter's reach, however, extends far beyond the high school walls and district lines. Named a 2013 NASSP Digital Principal, Carter's presence can be found throughout the blogosphere as a tech-savvy, innovative educator who writes, speaks, and learns through his PLN. It's not always easy.

"I used to get frustrated every day at work," recounts Carter. "I would start with a long to-do list of five or six items, and only complete *one* item. And then it hit me: I needed a shorter to-do list" (personal communication, July 24, 2013). He realized that sitting at his desk day after day, feeling defeated by his growing to-do list, was making him stagnate and keeping him from learning. Carter started to prioritize, completing one or two items a day and ramping up his efforts to engage students in class, teachers in the hallways, and parents in the office.

"Reflecting is at the heart of our profession," Carter says. "If we aren't reflecting, we aren't growing. I have chosen to reflect through writing my blog, for instance. It's for me. I'm not looking for reaction, or responses; writing helps me. Learning is key, and learning is mobile." To that last point, Carter adds, "learning must be 365 days a week, 24/7; for instance, if I have a few spare moments, I take time to connect with my Twitter feed. Instantly, I have educators speaking to me, I am reading current articles and education news, and I am learning, even if it is just for a few moments."

Carefully cultivating those few moments requires deliberate effort and savvy time management. To manage their time optimally, principals must first master the schedule.

Mastering the Schedule

The role of the leader is critical in helping the school realize its mission and vision in a timely manner. By building a unified calendar that focuses on the big picture of leadership and by prioritizing district, instructional, school, and community events and responsibilities in a balanced manner, school leaders can foster shared leadership and maximize participation and buy-in among the school community.

Synchronize the calendar. When principals who cannot master their schedules think about classroom walk-throughs, authentic conversations with teachers about professional goals, or pulse-taking meetings with parents, they sigh. They may think, *Sure, I'd love to do more of that … if I only had the time.* Time will pass, and they will give up on finishing that doctorate, sending off that article for publication, or writing that local grant to improve their school grounds. Their schools stagnate along with their practice.

It's time to stop saying, "I just don't have the time." There *is* time, but principals who use that excuse have failed to carve out their time in a proactive manner. Instead, they have let their time be devoured by *reactive* work.

The first step to mastering the schedule is to synchronize your calendar. It's vital to use *one* calendar. As a principal, I quickly learned to empower my office associates to place important items—parent meetings, scheduled check-ins from maintenance, fire drills—on my calendar. Most school leaders use a web-based calendar that synchronizes from the server onto a handheld device. Synchronize your personal items—birthdays, dentist appointments, soccer games—onto the calendar as well, since personal and work-related events often overlap (use privacy settings if you don't want your office staff to know about your second cavity in a semester!). Even the most effective principal can feel torn between a daughter's basketball game and the school dance, but planning ahead will help you maintain control over the calendar. Schedule monthly calendar meetings with office staff to ensure you are "synched" for success.

Review your calendar at the end of each day. Glance over the next day's events and consider how you can maximize your preparation for each. For instance, if you have a district-led principals meeting to attend, review the agenda items to prepare any updates or insights to share. If you have walk-through observations prioritized in a particular grade level or department, brush up on the pacing guide to consider what students are learning in those specific classrooms.

A four-point DISC perspective. There are four general categories of items that school leaders must prioritize in their master schedule, and they can be summed up by the acronym DISC: *district, instruction, school*, and *community*. Each of these key focus areas requires its own allocation of time and appropriate action.

- **District.** District items mandated by the central office include school-board hearings, principal meetings, leadership retreats, district subcommittees, and job recruitment fairs. Although any great principal is first and foremost an advocate for the school, district work is crucial to realizing results. Thus, principals must consider the district calendar before setting other calendar items. When you place district items on the calendar, adjust settings to ensure that you arrive 10 minutes early to the meeting or event. This small adjustment will enable you to make vital connections with district leaders and community members prior to the meeting and demonstrate that you are taking the meeting seriously.
- **Instruction.** Instruction-related calendar items are the heart and soul of a principal's work and include such events as grade-level or department professional

learning community (PLC) meetings, five-minute classroom walk-throughs, collaborative faculty meetings, and school-level committee meetings focused on student and staff success. Serving as the instructional leader requires intentional planning and collaborative action.

- **School.** School-centered events, activities, and celebrations help make the school the hub of the community. These can quickly overwhelm a principal who does not carefully incorporate them into the master schedule. It is important to maintain visibility in a healthy cross-section of school life, but a principal at any school level or size simply cannot attend them all. Prioritize!

- **Community.** Community items extend outside the boundaries of the school grounds. The principal has a powerful platform to engage and build partnerships with external entities, such as businesses, civic organizations, and social groups that can support the school, benefit *from* the school, appreciate its mission and vision, and provide ongoing insight and support. These unique partnerships require time and trust to cultivate and maintain.

Although Figure 1 (page 9) is not comprehensive, it provides a snapshot of how principals can incorporate recurring appointments into the calendar and consider time allocations for each. By setting the calendar in advance and using alerts, you are guaranteed to never forget a meeting. By inserting relevant "action notes" in the calendar as a reminder to arrive early, review the agenda, or prepare a short address, you can prepare to actively participate—rather than passively attend—important events, meetings, and opportunities.

Each of these DISC components should be seen as a recurring opportunity to sustain momentum in maintaining relationships and school improvement efforts. Building these items into the calendar as *proactive* opportunities still leaves plenty of time for the many items requiring *reactive* responses that continually crop up at the building level. Carving out time in advance will ensure that important priorities don't get lost in the mix.

Communicating Effectively

Once you have mastered the schedule, it's important to share it with stakeholders. Like you, these stakeholders have little time to waste. If your e-mails are lengthy and verbose and your "robocalls" to parents deliver a sermon-length to-do list, then you've effectively lost your audience. You are wasting your time—and certainly theirs—due to poor communication. Let's face it: most of our communication is about time. *Staff development will begin promptly at 2:00. Our student recognition assembly kicks off at 10:00.* Our main goal is to communicate an event's purpose and time briefly and concisely.

As I train future principals, work with teacher leaders, or engage with school staff members on school improvement work, I often see principal memos intending to share important information with the audience (usually teachers

FIGURE 1: **Monthly Master Schedule**

Item	Time	Action
Principal meeting	2nd Tuesday, noon–2:00 p.m.	Review agenda in advance and arrive 10 minutes early to discuss and collaborate.
School board meeting	3rd Wednesday, 6:00–8:00 p.m.	Be prepared to share school updates; bring calendar to note changes or additions.
Faculty meetings	1st and 3rd Wednesday, 2:45–4:15 p.m.	Work with leadership team each semester to organize agenda and action items.
Walk-through observations	At least 30 minutes per day (10 hours per month)	Conduct six walk-throughs each day, providing immediate feedback. Encourage sharing in faculty meetings.
Parent teacher organization meeting	1st Monday, 7:00–9:00 p.m.	Share principal update, listen to and discuss ideas, draft agenda for future events and fundraising efforts.
Fire drill	Once a month, varying day and time (10 minutes per month)	Review crisis procedure manual, record progress, reflect on response, plan for next steps.
Volunteer appreciation brunch	Final Tuesday of each semester, 10:00–11:00 a.m.	Highlight accomplishments, rotate short student performances, provide thanks and vision for next steps.
Business partnership outreach visit	Once a month for two hours	Visit three local businesses each month to discuss partnerships and sponsorships (e.g., "Student of the Week" gift certificates, "School Night" events at local restaurants).

and staff). Sometimes, these memos are thesis-length narratives that literally form a knot in my stomach. *What is the important takeaway here?* I wonder. *What actions will actually result from this memo?* Communicate that you value others' time, and you will lay a foundation for action and excellence in your school.

Communicate in innovative ways. Using innovative channels such as blogs and Twitter can help principals exponentially when it comes to communication. For example, principal Dwight Carter's blog, titled "Mr. Carter's Office" (http://dwightcarter.edublogs.org), provides a good model of how principals can communicate news and insights in an engaging way. Through his blog, Principal Carter shares insights on everything from the importance of staff expectations to a conference session he attended.

Principals can also benefit professionally from connecting and collaborating through Twitter and can model innovative sharing by inserting a school-based Twitter feed onto their school's home page. Twitter feeds enable schools to continually share successes, provide updates on events, and link to important announcements. School leaders seeking to innovate and collaborate in this manner might consider checking out Connected Principals (http://connectedprin cipals.com) to gain insights from school leaders in the field on how to share best practices and leadership ideas.

Schools have increasingly embraced robocalls as a way to instantly disseminate e-mail or voicemail updates to parents. Principals should ensure that these messages are concise—aim for a message that takes less than a minute to listen to or read—and make no more than three key points. As in a classic five-paragraph essay, introduce the three key points, expound briefly on each, and then repeat the key points again. Like it or not, we are communicators-in-chief, and we must always be "on" in this particular role.

The daily e-mail. E-mail is the primary mode of communication we use with faculty, but it's like fast food: fine in small doses, but too much of it can make you sick. Principals should carefully ration the e-mails they send to staff. My goal as principal was to consolidate everything important into one daily e-mail. Before I left to go home in the afternoon, I would sit at my computer and open my calendar to review the following day's events, meetings, and deadlines. I thought through the day's goals and considered important items and action steps to note in the message. Then I wrote and sent out the daily e-mail. In this way, I prepared both my staff and myself for the next day.

An effective e-mail is concise, bulleted, and reader-friendly. In *Insights into Action* (2011), I provide a sample daily e-mail that includes some of these key components:

- An initial greeting and the day's date.
- Highlights and achievements to share and affirm.
- Managerial items, such as fire drills or meeting times and locations.
- Schoolwide events, such as assemblies, athletic events, or field trips.
- Upcoming items to consider, such as Back-to-School night or an impending due date.
- An inspirational, relevant, and meaningful quote.

Taking time to end the day in a reflective moment and craft the e-mail for the following day helped me find balance as an assistant principal and principal. Staff members often told me how much they appreciated the consistency, and even inspiration, that this communication brought.

Reflective Questions on Managing Priorities

1. Do you own the master calendar in your school, or does it own you? How might you align the school calendar in a consistent, coherent manner that reduces confusion and maximizes participation and buy-in?

2. Consider the DISC priorities within your calendar. In which of these four areas do you need to invest more energy and time?

3. Open your school e-mail account's "sent" folder and reflect on all the e-mails you sent to your staff in the past week. What message and tone did these e-mails convey? How might you use the daily e-mail to consistently manage the school's daily calendar and set the tone for electronic communication?

4. After examining the communication approaches of Principal Carter (or another innovative leader on connectedprincipals.com), consider how you might use a blog to share insights, reflections, challenges, and successes with your school community.

A Time for Maximizing Learning

Today's schools are often "labeled" according to student achievement scores in reading and math. Nevertheless, our students receive, on average, only 76 minutes of English language arts (ELA) and 46 minutes of mathematics instruction per day (Phelps, Corey, DeMonte, Harrison, & Ball, 2012). The researchers note that "what stands out . . . are not the averages but rather the large variation across classrooms." Specifically, "a student in a classroom one standard deviation below the mean can expect to spend a daily average of 56 minutes less time in ELA instruction and 30 minutes less in mathematics instruction than a student attending the corresponding classroom one standard deviation above the mean" (p. 632). The gap seems astounding, but what the numbers are telling us is, sadly, not at all surprising: those who are learning less are being taught less, and those who are learning more are being taught more. We must ask ourselves, *Are we giving our students the time they need to learn?*

Of course, success must be defined in a much larger context than just reading and math scores, and our solution must entail more than simply upping the dose of "more of the same." We cannot add more seat time under fluorescent lights and expect more engaged students. In addition to all of that seat time's negative effects on engagement, there's our students' health to consider. As of 2009–2010, 69 percent of all students in the United States were considered obese or overweight (National Center for Health Statistics, 2012). Meanwhile, only 17–22 percent of all elementary schools offer daily physical education (Parsad & Lewis, 2006). Expanding our learning territory to include the outdoors, increased play, and healthy living would improve both student learning and engagement *and* students' health.

Educators can make a profound impact on learning by rethinking how they use time. A teacher who believes that student learning begins in the first second of class—not just when all the conditions are "right"—will likely have more engaged students. The principal who uses teacher input to shape the master schedule tends to put student learning at the forefront of how each day unfolds. This section explores the question *How can we maximize time spent in active, engaged learning?* Our goal is to bolster student learning not only to get high scores on end-of-year bubble tests but also in a way that encompasses the well-being of the whole student.

A Focus on Instructional Time

Through wise use of transition times and by recruiting teachers' help in crafting the school schedule, principals can maximize all students' learning experiences.

Transition times. During Todd Finn's first year as principal of New Hanover High School in Wilmington, North Carolina (known locally as the filming spot for *Dawson's Creek*'s Capeside High), he quickly noticed three ways time was being wasted. First, students and teachers alike were often late to school. Because the school is located in a busy urban area, parking was understandably a challenge, and staff members often missed getting to school by their on-duty time of 8:00 a.m. This in turn affected the instructional start time of 8:30 a.m., and as a result, much of the first hour was wasted. "Unfortunately, this set the tone for the rest of the day," Finn observes (personal communication, May 28, 2013). The second problem was that transitions between classes were a mess and "gave students permission to be loud, rowdy, and out of control for five to six minutes." Third, lunchtime was chaotic; each of the three lunch periods teemed with hundreds of the school's 1,650 students either waiting in line or sitting around with little purpose.

With key pockets of valuable instructional time being wasted, Finn knew that the school's culture was at risk. Data confirmed that most discipline infractions happened just before school, during lunch, or between classes. Finn decided to approach all three time hurdles in his first year. Although some strategic plans take years to reach fruition, school leaders can achieve certain "quick wins" in other areas (Duke, 2010). When it came to time management, New Hanover High was in need of quick wins.

First, Finn eliminated the system of allocating parking spaces by seniority (even relinquishing his own prime parking space) and instead implemented a "first come, first served" approach that granted the earliest teachers the best spots. Teachers were expected to be in their classrooms by 8:00, and students were permitted to enter their classrooms anytime between 8:00 and 8:30. Soon, a "hidden curriculum time" of tutoring, discussion, and interactive games became the new norm as teachers and students grew accustomed to arriving early and getting focused for learning. Finn makes the morning announcements promptly at 8:25, keeping them short—as he notes, "after two minutes, you've lost them!"—and simply sharing the school's vision and successes. Full morning announcements are posted online for all stakeholders to see, and teachers use projectors to scroll through them with students. This new morning announcement system maximizes time and relevance, and learning becomes the focus of morning transition time.

As his next step, Finn stopped using bells to signal transitions, instead empowering teachers to dismiss students at the scheduled times. This change immediately made hallway transitions, as Finn recounts, "more of a trickle effect and less of a 'running of the bulls.'" Teachers are now expected not to shut their doors in the faces of tardy students but instead to have a "face-to-face conversation" and invite them into the classroom. Students and faculty alike embraced this new change, which created more of a college-type atmosphere than the previous five minutes of uncontrolled chaos. Students took on personal responsibility to get from class to class without a bell, and teachers felt empowered to end class and prepare effective transitions in their own ways. In the end, hallway infractions plummeted and student engagement skyrocketed.

Finn's third move was to change the lunch schedule from three 40-minute lunch periods to five 25-minute lunch periods. Before he made this move, he gathered data: "We did a study of picking several random students in each of the different three long lunch periods and simply observing them and measuring how they spent their time." Finn noted that the average wait time in the lunch line was an astounding 22 minutes. The cafeteria was packed, "students were on top of each other," many did not have a seat, and the whole situation was a recipe for disaster. After adjusting the lunch schedule, the average lunch-line wait time fell to seven minutes, and every student was able to sit. Without needing to alter the total amount of time allotted for lunch in the school schedule, Finn's change led to a decrease in discipline incidents and was an immediate success.

These three changes, Finn notes, were perhaps "managerial" in scope, yet they had profound cultural implications, inviting students to participate as members of the school community. The students have risen to the challenge, and New Hanover's test scores have climbed steadily while discipline infractions have decreased substantially.

Elementary schools can also realize profound results by making better use of time and transitions. As Roxann Kriete (2002) points out in *The Morning Meeting Book*, having an established time for greeting, sharing, group activity, and a morning message of news and announcements from the teacher provides a "foundation for every lesson, every transition time, every lining-up, every upset and conflict, all day and all year long" (p. 3). Allocating time to revisit the school's mission, focus on achievements and next steps, and share with one another can bolster student learning and staff effectiveness.

Collaborative scheduling. As an elementary school principal, I realized that our master schedule would best serve our school if it were built collaboratively by teachers and kept student learning as the top priority (Sterrett, 2011). Schedules, like parking spots, are often overtaken by adult-centered priorities (such as seniority) rather than focused on students. The master schedule should not have just one author, and it should prioritize students and school improvement goals in an equitable manner. To make the best use of time, I suggest using a one-day retreat (giving participants release time and feeding them well!) to focus on crafting a schedule. Five important steps can help school teams organize their efforts:

Step 1. First, assemble a team that is small enough to work in an efficient manner but large enough to represent the diverse interests of the school. An elementary school team can work well with three members: one specials/arts teacher, one reading teacher, and one generalist or math teacher. For a middle school, including five teachers (one from each of the three grade levels, a specials/arts teacher, and a counselor) should be effective. A large high school would likely need a team of department heads, counselors, and an administrator familiar with credits and testing. Hold an initial meeting with the team to establish priorities, examine the school's current schedule and achievement data, look at the school's desired state (including the School Improvement Plan, or SIP), and set the tone by establishing norms, expectations on reaching agreements, and next steps. Then step back and entrust the committee to do its work.

Step 2. The team should first focus on achievement goals and related human resources (such as specialists, assistants, and tutors) to determine schedule "nonnegotiables." For instance, elementary schools that employ half-day teaching assistants may need to schedule their ELA instruction in the morning to allow for "all hands on deck" in facilitating breakout groups and reading rotations. Once those initial blocks are filled, the team can prioritize planning and instruction for other subject areas.

Step 3. The next step is to incorporate team planning time. For high schools, it is paramount to set weekly meeting times for department teams or PLCs. For middle school, both grade-level meetings to discuss specific students and subject-area PLC meetings focused on content have merit, so finding a way to do both should be prioritized if feasible. At the elementary level, having grade-level team meetings means that once a week, all students in a given grade should be in specials/arts at the same time (ideally, two back-to-back classes, such as art and library or music and P.E.) to facilitate a long-enough planning period.

Step 4. Next, the team should focus on instructional priorities. Many schools have clear SIP goals dedicated to reading and math achievement, for example, so the collaborative team should focus on scheduling these subjects at times when interruptions are minimal, students are primed for learning, and collaborative resources (specialists and assistants) are fully available. Thus, if a middle school principal in a rural district is grappling with student tardiness due to ongoing transportation issues, scheduling reading/

language arts for the first block could be detrimental. Likewise, it might not be wise for an elementary school to schedule a 60-minute math block immediately after lunch and recess; instead, the schedule could allocate time after the extended break for teachers to hold a short class meeting to clarify expectations for the learning to follow.

Step 5. After the team has drafted the schedule, several teachers who are not on the committee should have the chance to review it. Their feedback should go back to the scheduling committee for consideration. Then the committee should share the process and the result with the entire school and reiterate the school mission and improvement goals as paramount. Make sure to solicit ongoing staff input; using an online questionnaire tool such as SurveyMonkey (www.surveymonkey.com), for example, can help ensure that the committee receives accurate and anonymous feedback. Realizing that not everyone will always be happy with the schedule can be liberating to the committee, whose primary focus, after all, is on students and achievement goals. Ensuring that the schedule works first for students and then for staff in an equitable manner can pay large dividends in maximizing instructional time.

Time for the Whole Child

Just as important as the nuts and bolts of transitions and scheduling is incorporating all students' needs into the day. When schools take steps to build relationships and foster learning outside school walls, students will see that teachers, principals, and the entire school community truly have their best interests in mind. In turn, students will buy in to the notion that they can succeed in school.

Schoolwide mentoring program. In my third year as a principal, two teachers came to me with an idea. They realized that although many of our students had a particular teacher "assigned" to them—for example, students who were labeled as gifted or with special needs or who had a speech therapy or behavior plan—the vast majority of students did not have a particular teacher to check in on them. These two teachers' leadership served as a powerful catalyst in initiating a schoolwide mentoring program that was fueled by their ability to form and maintain strong relationships with students (Sterrett, Sclater, & Murray, 2011). Three steps helped get this effort off the ground.

First, the two teachers defined the program. They gave it a name (their acronym was COSTS—Connecting Our Students, Teachers, and Staff) and a purpose: they each wanted to be able to work with one specific student, on their own time (usually during lunch, a planning period, or before school during that "hidden curriculum" time identified by Principal Finn). They set an expectation of checking in with the student at least once each week. Then they shared their idea at a faculty meeting.

Next, the teachers took stock of the school's existing needs and resources. After gauging faculty interest, they made two lists: (1) students who needed a mentor and (2) staff who were willing to be mentors. They looked at available times and possibilities, asking questions such as *Would the student's homeroom teacher be willing to release him or her for a 20-minute break during my own lunch period?* They devised sample introductory talking points to help teachers connect with their mentees. They provided permission letters for each interested student to take home that apprised the students' parents of the program and its scope and format.

Third, the teacher leaders communicated with the mentors. Encouraging their colleagues to check in, sharing ideas and strategies that worked, and organizing one after-school field trip each semester (with administrative support of costs and transportation), such as a two-hour trip to the local apple orchard, helped instill a sense of community and consistency. The fact that the program was initiated by teachers rather than mandated by administrators was key in making this a successful initiative.

Committing to build positive, consistent relationships cannot be undervalued in a climate of increasing mandates and responsibilities. Teachers willing to carve out a regular 20-minute block and administrators willing to lead by example and allocate resources can realize enormous dividends in student growth. Measures of the COSTS program's success included positive student feedback and decreased discipline referrals. Teachers often remarked on how "their" students would seek them out to share a high grade on a test or invite them to attend their baseball game. Although relationships are difficult to measure, their impact is powerfully obvious to those in the school community.

Outdoor learning. In the ongoing discussion about improving education, most of us seem concerned principally with what happens *inside* schools. Our world, through technological advances, is becoming increasingly screen-centered and indoors-oriented, prompting some to ask, *Do our kids have nature-deficit disorder?* Richard Louv (2009) lauds what he calls "natural teachers" who "insist on taking their students outside to learn" (p. 25). Louv and countless other authors, researchers, health professionals, and educators point to mounting evidence that students stand to gain much from increased time outdoors. However, one excuse is often offered to the contrary: *We don't have the time to go outdoors.* Many students spend more time on the bus than in any sort of outdoor setting during school. We can learn something from Leo Politi Elementary School principal Brad Rumble and his faculty who infused an inner-city Los Angeles elementary school with a focus on nature learning. "Yes, funding is tight in California," Rumble notes, "but we realized that we had two resources with which we could be creative and make a difference: time and space" (personal communication, June 5, 2013).

As he assumed his leadership position in the Los Angeles Unified School District in 2008, Rumble realized that there were parts of the school grounds "we simply didn't use. I grew up someplace very different from inner-city L.A., and I kept having this gnawing feeling that something was missing in education—a connection to the natural world." He added, "When we are teaching about migration or habitat, there needs to be some background knowledge," which students lacked.

With the help of the Los Angeles Audubon Society, Rumble pursued a Schoolyard Habit Restoration Program grant through the U.S. Fish and Wildlife Service, which gave the school the funds to "take an outdoor space and turn it into a living laboratory for our children." The school team replaced asphalt and nonnative grasses with native flora, which then attracted native insects. "It was truly 'build it and they will come,'" Rumble notes. "Native insects came first. As soon as we planted the right things, lady beetles, all sort of butterflies like the Pygmy Blue, even solitary native leafcutter bees started to appear."

Resident and migrating bird species soon followed, prompting Rumble, an admitted birder, to organize "Bird Walks with the Principal" and assign writing activities to encourage student voice in different genres. For example, students could choose to write a personal narrative of an encounter with nature, an expository piece about a Western Meadowlark or Ash-throated Flycatcher, or a persuasive piece arguing why every school should have a space dedicated as a native habitat. This urban school of more than 800 students has been transformed. "About 300 of our students stay after school, and they're often learning about the outdoors," Rumble notes, "and our identified 'gifted' population has exploded to nearly 100 students" as students' learning about the outdoors has inspired their efforts in writing, exploration, and art. The results of this transformation, described in the *Los Angeles Times* as "remarkable" (Sahagun, 2012), are also evident in the school's significantly improved science test scores.

Even after finding space for outdoor learning, however, the most engaging school leader still faces time constraints. Rumble built a relationship with the Los Angeles Audubon Society, which involves local high school students in their educational initiatives, and he found resources to bring in part-time retired educators to facilitate lessons for 2nd and 3rd graders. A few key steps can make a profound difference in increasing outdoor learning time (Sterrett, 2011).

First, school leaders should conduct a schoolwide nature "audit" in which faculty, parents, and even students walk around the school grounds and share ideas for learning and activities that can occur outdoors. From leaf and insect identification to trust-building exercises or read-alouds, these ideas will help expand the boundaries of the school's current on-grounds best practices.

Second, the leadership team, school improvement team, vertical curriculum alignment committee, or other similar team should map out specific areas, themes, and outdoor spaces that align with teaching and learning for a particular grade level. At the elementary level, this might mean dividing up plots of a schoolyard garden based on different regions and their native plants. A secondary science team might maintain a wetlands area and encourage cranes to return home. This effort requires planning and teamwork to ensure that no single team or subject area dominates.

Third, the school leader should invite potential volunteers (parents, community members, and organizations willing to help in an ongoing or one-time capacity) to an orientation to share need-to-know details (e.g., how to sign in, current needs to be filled, background checks) and to brainstorm ideas and discuss the school's needs and volunteers' areas of expertise.

The school leadership team should also explore grant-writing initiatives at the local and national levels. The grant applications should demonstrate how the solicited resources will enhance outdoor learning and result in actual learning outcomes.

Finally, the team needs to find ways to share the good news about the outdoor learning initiatives. Pictures and updates on the school's website, press releases, and student work displayed throughout the school will communicate that outdoor learning is a priority and show how it is making a difference in the lives of students and staff. For example, the Leo Politi website (http://politi-lausd-ca.schoolloop.com) features students' nature projects, a column by Principal Rumble, and video testimonials about outdoors learning.

Reflective Questions on Maximizing Learning

1. Consider Principal Finn's assessment of how much time was wasted during hallway transitions and lunchtime. Consider his use of data to help inform his decision to use that time better. How might you use transition time in your school? What data points will guide your decision making?

2. As you reflect on your school's master schedule, what "sacred cows" are in place that make life easier for teachers but do not serve students? Consider which teachers you might recruit to your school's collaborative scheduling

committee. How might you and this team change the schedule to maximize instruction?

3. Consider how a schoolwide mentoring program would work at your school. Who would introduce it? What components would you emphasize (check-ins, semester events, etc.)?

4. How might your school invest more time in incorporating outdoor learning? How would you go about creating a nature track, a schoolyard learning garden, or outdoor learning spaces? What ideas do you have with regard to volunteers or grant funding?

A Time for Collaborative Growth

Faculty meetings. Teaching observations. Department or grade-level meetings. These are often met with a collective groan from teachers and—sadly—the principals who are trying to schedule and plan these meetings. Far from being seen as a catalyst for learning, they are largely viewed as a waste of time.

For many educators, any real, systemic "student teaching" concludes the moment they receive a teaching license and sign a teaching contract. But our own professional learning about teaching strategies, issues, and challenges should not stop the moment we become educators. We must continually hone our skills.

Principals often miss opportunities to use meetings and their leadership position to continually encourage "student teaching" and share out great teaching moments. Fortunately, time can be our greatest ally in fostering collaborative growth.

A Focus on Effective Teaching

The school leader knows better than anyone teachers' strengths and growth areas, and it is the school leader who owns, perhaps unfairly, the ultimate responsibility for realizing ongoing school improvement. By sharing this work collaboratively, however, the principal can turn faculty meetings and observations from file-drawer fodder to reflection and growth that affect staff and students alike.

Faculty meetings. The very notion of faculty meetings makes even some of the best teachers cringe. Asking the staff to convene at the end of a busy day is something that any school leader should carefully consider. Principals, take note: if you are struggling to come up with a reason to meet, make the wise decision and cancel the meeting. Be *inspirational*, not merely *informational*. School leaders should model what they want learning to look like in their buildings. A principal rambling through a laundry list of managerial items in a meeting is no different from a teacher passing out a dreaded "word find" worksheet to his or her class. As a rule of thumb, ask yourself, *If I were a teacher, would I want to attend this meeting?*

You can take several steps to ensure that teachers do not view faculty meetings as a complete waste of time (Sterrett,

2011). First, before the meeting, clarify expectations. Faculty members can better engage when there are agreed-upon parameters in place. Early in the school year, send out a schedule of meetings and, when possible, distribute an agenda prior to each meeting. Teachers will tune in better if they have an idea of what the meeting is about, and a brief outline will help them focus during the meeting. Asking a reflective question on the agenda (such as *How might we encourage student voice in our school improvement process?*) will help generate ideas in advance and foster buy-in: true engagement requires everyone to have a voice. Meeting facilitators should begin and end on time; when it's clear that everyone's time is seen as valuable, stakeholders will work harder to maximize it.

To make the best use of meeting time, focus on the *ABC*s of meetings: *affirmation*, *best practices*, and *coordination*.

- **Affirmation.** Start each meeting by recognizing others' successes and innovations. Principals are uniquely poised to share "what's right" with the school. Allowing teachers to recognize one another can go a long way toward creating a positive climate and high morale. Encourage teachers to take the time to recognize a colleague by reading aloud a note that sums up the colleague's successes and giving the colleague a gift card (as a principal, I worked with local business partners to keep gift cards handy). Consider rotating a symbolic object, such as a stuffed animal mascot or trophy, that allows teachers to "pass the torch" at the beginning of each meeting. These affirmations set the tone for meetings, and teachers actually begin to look forward to them!

- **Best practices.** To encourage best practices, share examples of what is working well within the school and discuss new opportunities for growth. When you conduct classroom walk-through observations, take short videos, first asking teachers if they would be willing to share insights about the clip in a future faculty meeting. Principals are in a position to leverage powerful insights from teachers and students, and sharing video clips of teaching and learning highlights can transform a faculty meeting's tone and level of involvement. Feel free to invite an occasional guest speaker or show a clip from a TED talk. Authentic, teacher-led discussion about actual teaching in the classroom will take engagement to another level.

- **Coordination.** Faculty meetings should be coordinated in such a way that they deliver results while allowing teachers to shape their course and scope. When I say *teachers*, I'm not just talking about teacher leaders, such as department or grade-level heads or mentors; it's also important to give a platform to teachers who have little experience or who don't hold an official leadership position. All teachers should engage in a discussion about curriculum, instruction, and next steps. One way you can facilitate broad participation is to use live Twitter feeds or sites such as http://todaysmeet.com to enable teachers to converse via "backchanneling" throughout the meeting. Monitor the backchannel comments, and periodically open discussion that addresses the typed conversation.

At the end of each meeting, be sure to outline what should happen next. Clear, well-thought-out action steps (e.g., *Each department will review and revise exit slips in their core subject area for the next three weeks* or *With a colleague, review these four teaching strategies and discuss your thoughts on student engagement*) will maintain the momentum of school improvement. Occasionally, use the scheduled faculty meeting time to let all teams conduct a deeper PLC-formatted meeting with specialists and administrators on standby to offer support.

End each meeting by soliciting participants' positive takeaways, constructive criticism, and further comments or questions, either through a short written exit slip or through a web-based survey tool. Pay attention to the staff feedback, and adapt accordingly. Teachers will notice when their principal is listening.

Peer observations. Few would deny that teachers have a deep desire to learn from one another. Principals can build on this desire by inviting teachers to engage in walk-through and sit-in observations of colleagues. Kachur, Stout, and Edwards (2013) note that both teachers and students gain from teachers' purposeful, collaborative participation in walk-throughs and peer observations. It's the role of the school leader to make time to facilitate this work.

Start by showing teachers a snapshot of what teaching and learning looks like in the building. For example, you could show a video clip from a walk-through observation in a faculty meeting, encouraging the filmed teacher to lead the discussion, as discussed above. Also consider asking a teacher to lead staff in an exercise demonstrating a new instructional strategy.

Teachers also need to look inside themselves for insight into their practice. Maya Angelou is quoted as saying, "I've learned that you shouldn't go through life with a catcher's mitt on both hands; you need to be able to throw something back." We must be willing to both "catch" (i.e., identify areas where we need development) and "throw" (i.e., share our strengths with colleagues). Principals can lead the way in affirming what individual teachers might share and helping to identify possible growth areas.

Next, principals need to carve out time for teachers to visit one another's classrooms. Peer observations shouldn't just occur during teachers' meager planning time or lunch breaks. Instead, either schedule short-term coverage to enable individual teachers to conduct peer observations or schedule a full-day substitute teacher to provide half-hour-long peer observation breaks for multiple teachers throughout the day, allowing teachers to observe a colleague's class during a meaningful and relevant time frame.

Finally, principals should encourage—and model—reflective feedback. Feedback is especially powerful when it comes from a colleague. Far from an "evaluative checklist," quality reflective questions encourage deeper reflection on and ownership of one's teaching practice. Examples include

- *I noticed James had his head down the entire period. What do you think is the cause of his behavior, and what could we do to help him?*
- *I saw over half of your students clamoring to use the interactive whiteboard, and a few just watching. How can you ensure that all students have the opportunity to engage?*
- *I noticed you spent a good deal of time on the "patterns" standard in your 5th grade math class. Do you have any advice for us 4th grade teachers on teaching our patterns strand?*

Teachers can share feedback with their colleagues through short notes or exit slips, or during one-on-one follow-up meetings. Principals do not need to see the questions or the responses but should support this collaborative dialogue. The key is to foster reflection and teachers' willingness to learn and grow.

A Focus on Collaboration

Today's principals are "professional developers-in-chief." With increasing mandates and ongoing budget challenges, this role isn't likely to change anytime soon. By encouraging teachers to take charge of their learning and cultivating time for teamwork, however, the school leader can realize increased collaboration and sustained school success.

PLC meetings. Lyn Hilt, an instructional technology coach and contributor to Connected Principals, notes that if school leaders "move away from talking about details that many teachers find redundant or irrelevant, we can instead focus on leadership and action that can impact the school, teams, and, ultimately, students" (personal communication, June 5, 2013). Hilt notes that by modeling smart use of technology, principals can help grade-level or department teams focus on what matters most—student learning—rather than managerial items that tend to be relevant only to a handful of adults. Here are a few ways, according to Hilt, to make team meetings more effective and efficient:

1. **Use an interactive online template for PLC minutes and feedback.** Using an online template enables teachers to enter and share team meeting data and principals or other instructional leaders to review and respond to the data. In many schools, grade-level or department teams submit weekly minutes that are based on guiding PLC questions, such as those posited by DuFour and Mattos (2013) that focus on learning, data, and next steps. Figure 2 provides an example of a possible template.

Hilt notes that "principals cannot be everywhere at the same time, but by creating and supporting a format that works, teacher leadership can emerge." For example, an interactive form such as the one in Figure 2, housed on Google Drive, could be accessed by the grade-level team and principal for ongoing dialogue and shared ideas.

FIGURE 2: **Interactive Online Template for PLC Minutes**	
Guiding Questions	**Possible Team Responses**
Content: What content, skills, and dispositions do we expect our students to learn?	(content area and skills to be covered)
Time: How much time will the unit, lessons, and strategies involve? Where does our work align with our curriculum map and pacing guide?	(curriculum map and pacing focus areas)
Data: What will inform us of student progress during and after student learning?	(formative assessment data, checking for learning and understanding)
Next steps: How can we continually improve teaching and learning? What will we do for students who have been successful in learning the content? What will we do for students who are struggling?	(next steps; ideas for remediation and enrichment)

2. **Model technology.** As a school leader, you have the opportunity to demonstrate, whether in a faculty meeting or as a coteacher, effective and innovative uses of technology in the classroom. For example, by demonstrating a new interactive whiteboard lesson, you can equip teachers with a new strategy. Another way to model smart use of technology is to create an official school blog, take time to promote it (on Back-to-School night, for example), and encourage teachers to start their own classroom blogs.

3. **Create structures to make work efficient and effective.** As principal, Hilt worked with staff to incorporate items such as the teacher's handbook or student data systems into a password-protected online database where staff could easily access needed information in a quick and secure manner. These steps require some work up front (e.g., setting up Google Drive for all teachers and organizing handbook information into a web portal), yet they ultimately give teachers more time to focus on what matters most: engaging students and growing as professionals.

Collaborative partners. For many of us, the only times we see other principals are at district meetings or professional conferences. Unfortunately, this perpetuates our tendency to work in silos and stifles our own growth and innovation. As principal, I coauthored an *Educational Leadership* article with a secondary-level principal about our collaborative partnership (Sterrett & Haas, 2009). Once a month, in the midst of a busy day, we would alternate visiting each other and block off at least an hour to exchange professional insights, conduct joint walk-through observations, or discuss ways to overcome challenges. This partnership was not sustained by accident but through intentional planning and prioritization.

We provide mentors for our novice teachers all the time, yet we often neglect to take care of ourselves in the same manner. I strongly recommend that school leaders identify a principal peer to serve as an accountability partner. Do not wait for a district-initiated program to make it happen. This colleague should preferably be in the same district to allow for shared vertical conversations and opportunities to overcome district challenges together. Then decide on a regular time to meet (e.g., 10:00–11:30 on the first Wednesday of every month) and build it into the calendar as a sacred appointment. Rotate hosting duties to maximize shared experiences and perspectives. The host principal can send out a reminder and a topic to think about in advance, such as

- Curriculum and instruction changes or success stories.
- Ideas and action steps gleaned from a recent professional article or book.
- Application of or opportunities stemming from a district initiative.
- Conference or professional development takeaways or effective staff development ideas.
- Plans to collaborate on a conference presentation or coauthor an article.

Reflective Questions on Collaborative Growth

1. Consider the faculty meeting *ABC*s. How might you better prioritize affirmation of staff qualities or accomplishments, recognize and share best practices, and coordinate next steps in a targeted fashion?

2. Arrange time for teachers to observe one another's classes. How might you foster a collaborative approach to peer observations by better engaging your teachers in this work?

3. How might you incorporate consistency, teacher autonomy, and shared leadership into grade-level or subject-area PLC meetings?

4. What are your goals in working with a collaborative partner? What are your first steps in ensuring that this partnership is sustained and helpful to both of you?

Making Time

Where did you find the time to write that article?

I didn't know you had finished your doctorate—congratulations!

It's great to see your students learning outdoors; we need to find the time to do that at our school.

Imagine hearing these statements from principal colleagues or community members. These goals, and many more, are within our reach. We have the time. *You* have the time.

Odds are you took precious time to read this publication because you realize your potential to do even more as a leader. Now the ball is in your court. You have a game plan; it's time for *action*. What will your next steps be?

How can you invest minutes today that yield hours of opportunity tomorrow? How can you master your calendar to help you connect better with your school community and district leaders? Imagine doubling the amount of outdoor learning so that when your students think of school they think of flora and fauna instead of bubble tests and fluorescent lights. Envision holding faculty meetings that staff members look forward to attending each month. Consider the gains you stand to realize by having consistent, uninterrupted time for collaboration with a principal colleague each month.

As a school leader, you have the profound opportunity to reach new goals—but it won't happen by accident. Use your calendar wisely, and make the time to keep learning and growing as a leader. Your school depends on it.

Acknowledgments

I would like to acknowledge several educators in the field who provided valuable insights on their work as leaders and learners: Dwight Carter, Todd Finn, Lyn Hilt, and Brad Rumble. Thank you for speaking to the importance of maximizing time to realize greater success for schools, students, and staff alike.

I would also like to thank the wonderful team of editors at ASCD who encouraged and supported me in this work: Genny Ostertag, for her initial perspective and helpful advice, and Miriam Goldstein, for her attention to important details and refinement of the end product.

To give your feedback on this publication
and be entered into a drawing for a
free ASCD Arias e-book, please visit
www.ascd.org/ariasfeedback

ENCORE

GETTING STARTED: 18 TIMELY ACTION STEPS

You can find additional action steps online at www.ascd.org/ASCD/pdf/books/Sterrett2013Arias.pdf.

BEGINNING TO LEAD

1. Convene the school improvement team prior to the beginning of the school year to examine data, current goals, and current challenges. Envision how to continue, improve, or replace these goals. Ensure maximum stakeholder input from teams, departments, parents, and students. Review and consider updates to the current handbooks, schedules, rosters, and crisis plans.

2. Review budget priorities and procedures and schedule a specific meeting with a district leader (and your assistant principal[s], if relevant) to overview current states, priorities, and next steps. Review personnel files and consider any existing improvement plans, hiring opportunities, or impending changes.

INSTRUCTIONAL LEADERSHIP

1. Meet regularly with teams to review current standards, curriculum, assessment (formative and summative), and teaching strategies.

2. Protect instructional time. Continually monitor—and reduce—interruptions and distractions that interfere with learning, engagement, and planning.

INNOVATION

1. Continually explore ways to integrate technological innovations into your school's practice. For example, consider incorporating Quick Response (QR) codes into learning, facilitating interactive exit slips or scavenger hunts, using handheld devices in class for learning-based interactions, and connecting with students and educators in other countries to enhance global perspectives.

2. Before adopting a schoolwide innovation initiative (e.g., interactive whiteboards or a 1:1 tablet program) consider how it will affect learning and whether your school community is willing to commit the time and energy needed to do it right. Do your research as a planning committee and look for examples of schools that have successfully made similar investments.

SCHOOL CULTURE

1. Consider the vision statement of your school. With your school improvement team, consider how you might better lead, live, and share the vision each day. How might

you increase buy-in of the vision and make more progress toward achieving your SIP goals?

2. Do not let your school be defined solely by end-of-year test results that measure only "outputs." With your improvement team, help define—and continually and consistently refer to—other success points, such as improved attendance, decreased discipline incidents, student or staff innovation, grants received, or successful events.

SCHOOL–COMMUNITY PARTNERSHIPS

1. Invite your local congressperson to make a 30-minute visit to your school. Use school letterhead to write the invitation, and list three to five unique key points that define your school.

2. Research and sign up for organized annual volunteer drives to recruit volunteers to help meet your school's specific needs (e.g., painting or garden maintenance). Build and sustain these partnerships. Write personalized thank-you notes to recognize volunteers' contributions, and invite them to school events.

PROFESSIONAL AND STAFF DEVELOPMENT

1. Send teachers to conferences with one specified goal (e.g., learning about math differentiation or a new technology), but also encourage exploration and inquiry. Ask them to share at least one insight they gained at the next faculty meeting.

2. Encourage the rotation of team leaders or department chairs every few years and facilitate other team leadership roles to maintain shared leadership.

OUTDOOR LEARNING

1. Read Richard Louv's *Last Child in the Woods* (2008) and consider how outdoor learning might affect your particular school. Consider possibilities for outdoor learning at your school and next steps you need to take to make it a reality.

2. Conduct a faculty meeting outdoors. During the meeting, make a list of every potential outdoor learning space and brainstorm various learning activities that can occur outside. Make this list available to faculty.

SCHOOL MANAGEMENT

1. Be consistent and equitable when assigning morning, lunch, and after-school duties. Do not have favorites, and assign yourself a duty (you should be prominent at each of these times) that allows you to take stock of overall coverage and efficiency. Continually emphasize safety, transitions, and an adult presence.

2. Ride the buses after school (a different route each day until you have ridden all the routes) to learn the routes, neighborhoods, and stops. At each stop, quickly exit the bus and wave to parents to show you value safety and smooth operations.

THE WHOLE CHILD

1. Pay close attention to student hunger in your school, particularly on Mondays or after vacations. Observe student behavior and listen for comments regarding hunger. Act on possibilities to help reduce hunger in your school community, enlisting your district leaders, local community and faith-based groups, and business partners.

2. When conducting walk-through observations, zero in on students' perspectives. Ask students, "What are you learning? What excites you about this class?" Share insights with teachers, and figure out ways to act on student feedback.

References

DuFour, R., & Mattos, M. (2013). How do principals really improve schools? *Educational Leadership, 70*(7), 34–40.

Duke, D. L. (2010). *Differentiating school leadership.* Thousand Oaks, CA: Corwin Press.

Kachur, D. S., Stout, J. A., & Edwards, C. L. (2013). *Engaging teachers in classroom walkthroughs.* Alexandria, VA: ASCD.

Kriete, R. (2002). *The morning meeting book.* Greenfield, MA: Northeast Foundation for Children.

Louv, R. (2008). *Last child in the woods: Saving our children from nature deficit disorder.* Chapel Hill, NC: Algonquin Books.

Louv, R. (2009). Do our kids have nature-deficit disorder? *Educational Leadership, 67*(4), 24–30.

MetLife. (2013). *The MetLife survey of the American teacher: Challenges for school leadership.* Available: https://www.metlife.com/assets/cao/foundation/MetLife-Teacher-Survey-2012.pdf

National Center for Health Statistics. (2012). *Health, United States, 2011: With special feature on socioeconomic status and health.* Hyattsville, MD: Author. Available: http://www.cdc.gov/nchs/data/hus/hus11.pdf

Parsad, B., & Lewis, L. (2006). *Calories in, calories out: Food and exercise in public elementary schools, 2005* (NCES 2006–057). Washington, DC: National Center for Education Statistics.

Phelps, G., Corey, D., DeMonte, J., Harrison, D., & Ball, D. L. (2012). How much English language arts and mathematics instruction do students receive? Investigating variation in instructional time. *Educational Policy, 26*(5), 631–662.

Sahagun, L. (2012, April 16). Just attracting, naturally. *Los Angeles Times.* Available: http://articles.latimes.com/2012/apr/16/local/la-me-bird-school-20120416

Sterrett, W. (2011). *Insights into action: Successful school leaders share what works.* Alexandria, VA: ASCD.

Sterrett, W., & Haas, M. (2009). The power of two. *Educational Leadership, 67*(2), 78–80.

Sterrett, W., Sclater, K., & Murray, B. (2011). Preemptive relationships: Teacher leadership in strengthening a school community. *Virginia Educational Leadership, 8*(1), 17–26.

Related Resources

At the time of publication, the following ASCD resources were available (ASCD stock numbers appear in parentheses). For up-to-date information about ASCD resources, go to www.ascd.org. You can search the complete archives of Educational Leadership at http://www.ascd.org/el.

ASCD Edge©
Exchange ideas and connect with other educators interested in various topics, including Elementary Schedules and For Principals by Principals on the social networking site ASCD Edge at http://ascdedge.ascd.org.

Print Products
100+ Ways to Recognize and Reward Your School Staff by Emily E. Houck (#112051)

The Art of School Leadership by Thomas R. Hoerr (#105037)

The Big Picture: Education Is Everyone's Business by Dennis Littky and Samantha Grabelle (#104438)

Building Teachers' Capacity for Success: A Collaborative Approach for Coaches and School Leaders by Peter A. Hall and Alisa Simeral (#109002)

Engaging Teachers in Classroom Walkthroughs by Donald S. Kachur, Claudia Edwards, and Judith A. Stout (#113024)

Insights into Action: Successful School Leaders Share What Works by William Sterrett (#112009)

Leadership Capacity for Lasting School Improvement by Linda Lambert (#102283)

Leading Effective Meetings, Teams, and Work Groups in Districts and Schools by Matthew J. Jennings (#107088)

The New Principal's Fieldbook: Strategies for Success by Harvey B. Alvy and Pam Robbins (#103019)

School Leadership That Works: From Research to Results by Robert J. Marzano, Timothy Waters, and Brian McNulty (#105125)

ASCD PD Online© Courses

Schools as Professional Learning Communities: An Introduction (#PD09OC28)

What Works in Schools: School Leadership in Action (2nd Ed.) (#PD11OC119)

Leadership for Contemporary Schools (#PD09OC07)

Leadership: Becoming a Leading School (#PD09OC43)

Leadership: Effective Critical Skills (#PD09OC08)

For more information: send e-mail to member@ascd.org; call 1-800-933-2723 or 703-578-9600, press 2; send a fax to 703-575-5400; or write to Information Services, ASCD, 1703 N. Beauregard St., Alexandria, VA 22311-1714 USA.

About the Author

William Sterrett is an educational leadership faculty member and program coordinator at the University of North Carolina Wilmington. A former principal and teacher, he is the author of the 2011 ASCD book *Insights into Action: Successful School Leaders Share What Works.* He may be reached at the Watson College of Education, 601 South College Road, Wilmington, NC 28403; via e-mail at sterrettw@uncw.edu; or on Twitter: @billsterrett.